A

Bread

recipes for the old,
traditional wholegrain
wheat, barley and rye
breads of Wales, adapted
for baking today by

Bobby Freeman

FOOD and drink in Wales in the old days was of a style which today we would term a 'health food' diet, though it was dictated by circumstance and climate rather than a desire to rectify the habits of urban affluence.

It was a style of eating based largely on grains — oats, barley, rye and wheat — root vegetables, buttermilk and a limited amount of meat. It bred a healthy race of men and women with the strength and stamina to spend long hours in the fields and to withstand the cold, damp conditions of the uplands.

Bacon was the meat most usually eaten. Every cottager could keep a pig or two; the fatty bacon thus produced was relished for the protection it gave against the cold . . . in those days, when people were active both inside and outside the house, animal fat was not the danger to health it poses today.

The healthful aspects of what tended to be a rather monotonous diet is revealed by these lines on 'The Old Ways', by Eifion Wyn, which translated from the Welsh read:

'Let us all join in singing the praises of the old
    foods of Wales,
Oat and barley bread, porridge, whey and
    flummery.
What is more tasty and better for strengthening
    muscles
Than white sowans and brewis and yellow shot?
Let us believe, like our grandfathers, that the best
    medicine
Is camomile and wormwood, first thing every
    morning.
That rosemary and other herb teas will prolong
    one's life in town and country
All such inexpensive remedies.'

And in 'Old Memories', Sir Henry Jones wrote: 'But neither on Sunday nor on a week-day was the meal scanty, or the fun and chatter lean, or was there any faintest hint of scarcity or poverty . . . And the bread was of my mother's own making – the best in all the land!'

Sadly, many of the old concepts of healthy eating were lost when cheap sugar and chemical raising agents were introduced in Wales at the same time as many Welsh people left the land in search of work in the mining and ironworks towns. More latterly, the efficient spread of standardised food has eradicated much of the Welshness from the food of Wales. This of course includes what the multiple bakeries are pleased to call 'bread'.

Good bread, baked by family bakers in old-fashioned ovens, lasted a long time in rural Wales . . . twenty years ago, when I first came to Wales, I lived next door to one of those family bakeries, and the smell of fresh bread which greeted each early morning was one of life's particular joys.

Many of these family bakeries are still in business – and not just in rural Wales but in the industrial cities, too – baking good crusty bread in a variety of shapes and styles. And now the return of real 'brown' bread is under way, more and more of these bakeries are baking a genuine wholewheat loaf.

Wholegrain flours are once more being milled in Wales, in carefully restored water-powered mills by slow, stone-grinding which preserves the precious wheat-germ intact. There's a steady return to home-baking from these flours, and as the movement towards real bread gains momentum, to home*style* baking in some of the smaller bakeries.

Today, it's possible to make many of the old wholesome breads, on which the Welsh used to rely for strength and sustenance, now that wholegrain

THE MILL AT WHITEMILL,
NANTGAREDIG, NEAR CARMARTHEN

flours, including barley and rye, are readily available from specialist grain and health food shops. Even supermarkets now sell stoneground wholewheat and wheatmeal flours, some in their 'own brand' packs at considerable price savings.

Used with discretion and mixed with 'strong' flours, barley and rye produce interesting, delicious and nourishing bread.

In earlier times, right up to the end of the 18th century, the Welsh baked bread from barley flour. 'Better barley bread and peace than white bread and discord' ran the old Glamorgan ploughman's saying.

But barley bread was heavy (for barley contains little gluten and thus gives a poor rise); its value lay in its sustaining quality. It was often used in Wales to make thin, flat 'loaves' on the bakestone (griddle). These resembled leather and were in fact used as 'plates' for food, afterwards eaten if the food they had supported had been inadequate.

Bread made from rye flour was eaten without much enjoyment for its supposed medicinal qualities.

To grind the corn, there were little corn mills on the banks of all Wales' fast-flowing rivers and streams . . .mills just big enough to supply the immediate neighbourhood with barley meal, wheat flour and oatmeal. One of these has been re-erected at the Welsh Folk Musuem, St Fagan's, near Cardiff, and there are to my knowledge eight other working flour mills in Wales today, stone-grinding by water power: at Pentrefoelas near Blaenau Ffestiniog; Felin Geri at Cwm Cou, Newcastle Emlyn in Ceredigion; Y Felin at

OATCAKES 'BIG AS DINNER-PLATES' DRYING
BEFORE THE FIRE ON THEIR SPECIAL RACK.

Welsh Folk Museum. St Fagan's.

St Dogmaels, Cardigan; Felin Isaf at Glan Conwy, N. Wales; New Mill at Pumpsaint in Carmarthenshire; near Pontypridd and in Gwent. A ninth, and the oldest in Wales — The Mill at Whitemill, Nantgarcdig, near Carmarthen — has unbelievably had to convert to diesel power because the Water Authority wanted too much for the use of the river water.

There were windmills, too, particularly in Anglesey and in the Vale of Glamorgan; and there were a few tide mills — near Milford Haven in Dyfed a typical tide mill of the area is preserved at Carew.

While the growing of cereal crops may have been confined almost exclusively to the fertile valleys of Wales, the existence of corn mills in the narrow valleys of the moorlands — where conditions were completely unsuitable for cereal-growing — indicates that even there the sheep farmer grew enough oats, rye and barley for the family and animals.

'In my childhood we took the oats, the wheat and the barley to the local mill, and after discussion with the miller, we arrived at the exact kind of fineness best suited to our taste, and the exact amount of husk, if any, to be left in the final product.' James Williams, remembering Edwardian times on the family farm at Pen-y-bryn, near Cardigan, in *Give Me Yesterday*, 1971. (Gomer Press)

The old breads in Wales were mostly rough — coarse, even — made from wholewheat flour, barley-meal and oatmeal and rye flour. It often required great skill and ingenuity to produce acceptable bread in quite primitive conditions. Sometimes bread was baked in the wall oven, or in a bread oven housed in a separate little building across the yard from the house.

Or, in areas where peat was used for fuel, it was baked in the *ffwrn fach* – little pot oven – a large cast-iron pot with a lid. It worked on the principle of heat below and on top: the pot stood on a tripod over the indoor fire of red-hot peat, or over a similar fire built out of doors in a sheltered spot. Either way, the inside of the pot was greased, the bread dough placed inside, and glowing peat coals heaped on top of the lid. White bread – 'gentry bread' and therefore considered a great treat – was usually baked in the *ffwrn fach*.

FFWRN FACH

Quick breads of all kinds were baked on the bakestone. In some places the bakestone was made to work in a similar way to the *ffwrn fach* — the dough was placed on the heated bakestone which would have stood on a tripod over an indoor or outdoor fire of gorse or straw, then covered with an inverted cast-iron pan on to which glowing embers were heaped.

New cast-iron bakestones can be bought in craft shops and country hardware stores in Wales. Secondhand ones can sometimes still be found in antique shops, though the prices asked are often a bit steep.

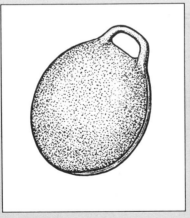

BAKESTONE
(planc, maen, llechwen, gradell)

ASSESSING THE QUALITY OF
THE GRAIN
(Welsh Folk Museum)

10

What you need to know about bread-making

Advice and information to help the recipes which follow.

BREAD-MAKING is much simpler than most people imagine, and working with yeast a lot less chancy than is popularly supposed. The essential thing is not to be afraid of it. Be prepared to make two or three batches of loaves in fairly quick succession so you become proficient in a very short time. Making the same thing over and over again is the key to success in every branch of cookery.

Next, think how successfully household bread was baked in the past in relatively primitive conditions ... and how in comparison the methods of the multiple bakeries in the production of their so-called 'bread' seem even more lamentable.

Baking bread at home is both satisfying and rewarding – from the initial frothing into life of the yeast and the sight of a bowlful of proudly swollen, spongy dough when it has created the first rise, to when the house is filled with the good smell of baking bread.

Although the whole process of breadmaking can take several hours, it is not time-consuming in terms of the time spent actually preparing and handling the dough. During the rising periods it is quite capable of looking after itself while you are doing something else – it can even be left alone in the house! Even those working a hectic, full-time week can fit bread-making into a weekend routine. For me, Saturday morning, when I set my dough to rise, is the most looked-forward-to part of the week. But when time on baking day is short, a long, cool, overnight rise is a useful alternative.

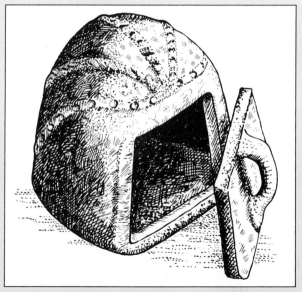

EARLY CLAY WALL OVEN, 16 x 16in,
FROM A GLAMORGAN FARMHOUSE

A dough-hook attachment on the electric mixer cuts kneading time down dramatically, but of course eliminates what can be the very positive pleasure of handling the dough.

There are no rigid rules in break-making and recipes vary widely. Find ones you like, experiment, but most important of all, get to know the feel of good, elastic dough.

What bread-making needs from beginning to end is the gentle warmth of the kitchen — and a good, quick heat when at length it goes into the oven. After about 20 minutes baking the heat can be lowered slightly, for bread is best baked on a falling heat: the old wall-ovens were heated by a fire lit inside them, which was then raked out and the bread put in.

INTERIOR, ARCHED BRICK OVEN

FLOUR TROUGH, POPTY'R LAWNT,
THE FORMER BAKERY AT DOLGELLAU

SALT

I have put this first, even before yeast because it is so
essential to the flavour of bread. Many home bakers
don't use enough and the result is a flat tasting loaf.
But the balance must be right as too much salt will
create a tough crust — those who like such a crust
should glaze their loaves with salt and water. Also,
the action of salt upon yeast is to slow the rise down,
so allow extra time if you increase the salt in a
recipe. Don't add salt to the yeast mixture directly or
it will kill the yeast completely. I prefer to dissolve
the salt in a little hot water before adding to the rest
of the tepid liquid for mixing the flour. Always use
sea salt which is free from additives and has a better
flavour than processed salt. If a hard crust has
resulted from too much salt being used in the bread
mix, wrapping the loaf while still hot from the oven
in a thick cloth will soften it.

YEAST

Use fresh, if you can get it, or dried (granule), which
is easily obtainable in health shops and most grocery
counters. Fresh yeast can be stored in a freezer for
several weeks. Dried yeast keeps almost indefinitely,
closely sealed, in a cool, dry place. I find it so
convenient, and the results so satisfactory, that I
have stopped hunting for sources of fresh yeast, and
use it all the time. But dried yeast needs a
teaspoonful of sweetener to bring it to life — I use
honey or dark brown molasses sugar. Sprinkle it on
to a little warm (100°F) water in which the sweetener
has been dissolved, whisk it round with a fork and set

POPTY'R LAWNT (LAWN BAKERY),
DOLGELLAU

16

aside in a warm place for 10 minutes or so, when it should be nice and frothy. If it fails to activate and feels cold, put it in a warmer place (like the oven turned on at lowest) but don't overheat or the yeast will be killed off. Yeast is a living organism and 'feeds', i.e. grows, on the sugar and protein in the flour. Once it has been added to the dough it produces carbon dioxide gas and this is what makes the dough light and spongey. What finally holds the gas in the bread is the gluten in the flour.

Some recipes activate the yeast by the 'sponge' method. This entails pouring the yeast and tepid water/sweetener mixture into a well made in the centre of the warmed flour. A little flour is sprinkled over the top and the bowl set aside, again for 10 minutes or so, until the yeast is frothy. I find the first method is the most satisfactory, but Mr Williams, whose modern bakery at Wem on the Welsh border in Shropshire makes lovely old-fashioned bread, recommends a 'flying ferment' for guaranteed success. For this, take enough of the flour to beat into a batter with the yeast mixture, set aside for 20 mins. It must sponge up and fall back – make your dough when it has fallen back, Mr Williams says.

FLOUR

The hard wheats grown in sunnier climates than ours used to be considered the best for bread. But long ago, before imports, we used home-grown wheat for our bread! Recently, Wales has been in the forefront of successful experiments with new strains of hard wheat suitable for our climate – now at the Cookery

FELIN GERI FLOUR MILL, CWM COU,
NEWCASTLE EMLYN

Centre I can make my Welsh breads from flour grown in Wales and stoneground at my local mill across the river in St Dogmaels.

Pimhill also uses exclusively British wheat.

Unless you like a rather dense, heavy loaf, it's advisable to mix a small proportion of strong plain white flour with most of the wholewheat flours.

'Hard' means 'strong' — that is, a high gluten content which is what holds the 'air' in the baked bread.

The flours available for breadmaking present a complex and often confusing picture because of the diversity of terms used on their labels. Extracting the information you require can be akin to reading the label on a bottle of wine. I will try to define the essentials as simply as possible. What you need to look for are three basic descriptions:

> plain white unbleached strong flour
> plain brown strong flour (see 'wheatmeal')
> 100% wholewheat/meal flour.

Unbleached white flour is a pale, creamy colour. It has not been subjected to the damaging bleaching process to make it whiter than white.

Wheatmeal flour, of an extraction rate of 81% or 85% of the grain, is nutritionally the next best thing to wholewheat flour and preferred by many for its lighter quality. All the essential wheat germ is there, but not all the bran, some of which will have gone for cattle food, or to sell separately. There maybe some additives – chalk, iron , vitamin B$_1$ and nicotinic acid. By itself it makes a nice, nutty flavoured loaf and is useful for mixing with other, low-gluten flours, such as rye and barley, as it is usually classified as a strong flour.

Wholewheat flour, if stoneground or *slowly* roller-milled (as with 'Jordan's') is 100% of the grain. This is the best (nutritionally) flour of all – nothing taken away, nothing added – and wholefood zealots will use no other, even for cakes and pastry, which I think is carrying things too far. But adding a small proportion of wholewheat flour to the softer flours which have been developed for confectionery often adds great charm to the taste of the pie or cake. The life-containing wheat germ is killed by the heat

CHECKING THE FACE OF THE STONE
DURING DRESSING
(Welsh Folk Museum)

21

generated in the fast roller-milling processes developed by the giant millers, but in any case they do not want it in their flour as the oil it contains shortens its storage life. So buy wholewheat flour in small quantities and don't try to keep it for long.

Bread made from wholewheat flour is very satisfying, and though an expensive flour, in the long run it is an economy, as less is eaten.

MIXING

Always warm the bowl and the flours first. (Put them in a very low oven and stir the flour around from time to time until warm all through). A little fat or oil added to the flour will produce a richer, long-keeping bread — if using butter or other hard fat, rub it in at this stage, and add dry salt now. Whether you use

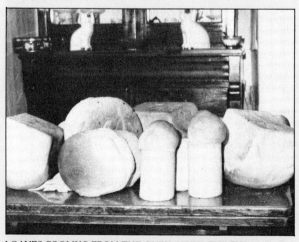

Welsh Folk Museum, St Fagan's.

LOAVES COOLING FROM THE OVEN. NOTE THE TWO 'DOLLY LOAVES' BAKED IN EARTHENWARE JAM POTS FOR THE CHILDREN — A CHARMING CUSTOM IN MEIRIONNYDD,

the 'sponge' method or froth the yeast first, always dabble the dough together with the figures of one hand, gradually incorporating the flour from around the sides of the well until the dough leaves the bowl clean. Add more liquid or flour as dictated. When handling dough which is sticky, flour the hands not the dough.

KNEADING

This is essential to create a smooth, elastic dough which will rise to give a bread with a fine, even texture. Kneading uses the palms of the hands in a stretching, pulling, folding, turning process. The first kneading usually takes 10-15 minutes by hand, 2 minutes on speed 2 with a dough hook on an electric mixer. Cover the dough to keep draught-free while it is set to rise with an oiled polythene sheet, or a damp cloth if you prefer being old-fashioned. Dough will take 45 minutes to an hour to rise in a warm place, two hours at average room temperature, 12 hours overnight in a cool room or larder, 12-14 hours in the refrigerator. The longer the rise the stronger the dough and the better the bread. Rising is complete when the dough has doubled in size and springs back when pressed with a gentle finger. Cool-raised dough should be brought up to room temperature before re-kneading. Before the second kneading 'knock' the dough back to its original size with the fist before kneading again for five minutes or so. Recipes which omit a second kneading and rise result in a heavier bread with a closer texture, which does not keep very long. Have your bread tins ready greased, floured and warmed.

Shape the dough for the baking sheet or tins (keep folds underneath) and set to rise or 'prove' (that the yeast is still alive) until it reaches the tops of the tins or doubles again.

BAKING

Bread takes 30-40 mins. according to the size of loaf. It should go into a quick oven to kill the yeast and so prevent over-rising and collapse – professional bakers know exactly how to catch the last of the rise in the first heat of the oven by astute judgement of the final proving in the tins; home bakers can acquire it, too. The richer, wholegrain breads need a slightly less hot oven than plain white or mixtures. When the loaf sounds hollow when tapped underneath, the bread is done. Slip it out of the tins and return to the cooling oven for a few minutes for a crisp all-round crust.

Mr Williams, the baker at Wem, recommends pre-heating a gas oven for at least 20 mins before using it for baking bread, so the sides and top will be well-heated and retain heat in the manner of the old brick or cast-iron ovens. And place a baking-tin of water at the bottom of the oven to create some steam to improve the baking.

THE WHOLEFOOD CONCEPT: if you like to keep your breadmaking within this, use honey or molasses sugar as a starter for your yeast, and vegetable or corn oil instead of hard fat – add it to the tepid liquid for best results.

The Recipes

Note:
though these recipes are based upon
original old Welsh breads, they are
adaptations and not traditional. A collection
of these appears in 'First Catch Your Peacock
– A Book of Welsh Food' by the
same author.

Yeast Breads

Wholewheat Bread
Bara Gwenith

2lbs wholewheat flour
2 teaspoons dried yeast dissolved with scant teaspoon honey or molasses sugar
2 generous teaspoons sea salt
1 tablespoon oil or 1 oz butter
1 pint warm water
METRIC: 900g flour; 575mls water

A satisfyingly chewy, richly-flavoured bread. For a lighter,
less dense loaf, use 1½lbs wholewheat flour and
½lb plain white strong flour.

Mix the frothed yeast into the flour with the remainder
of the warm water to which you've
added the oil and salt and work into a dough.
Knead until strong and elastic. Set to rise. Knock back and
knead again. Divide and place in tins, leave to rise for
about an hour until the dough reaches the top of the tins.
Bake in a fairly hot oven, lowering heat after 20 mins
for a total of about 45mins.

Barley Bread
Bara Barlys

1½ lbs barley meal
1 tablespoon salt
1 tablespoon dried yeast mixed with *2 teaspoons molasses sugar* *or honey in warm water.*
1 tablespoon vegetable oil
16 fl. ozs tepid water
METRIC: 675g barley meal; 450 mls water.

An acceptable all-barley meal loaf is not easy to make unless you are prepared to use a lot of yeast. I find this loaf a pleasant change from wholewheat, for the scent and flavour of barley are very attractive.

You can also experiment with 1lb barley meal and ½ lb plain white strong flour and the usual amount of yeast which will give a tight-textured loaf which is nice with cheese.

Mix the frothed yeast into the warmed meal, to which you have added the salt. Add the oil to the warm water and mix to a dough. Knead well and set to rise in a warmer place than usual – about 1½–2 hours, until doubled in size. Knock back, knead again, place in a large (3 pint) but not too deep tin and set to prove for up to an hour, covered, in a warm place. Make a deep cut along the top of the loaf and open it out with the side of your hand before putting in to bake in a fairly hot oven for approximately 1 hour. Sprinkle the top with sesame seeds if liked before baking.

Barley and Wheatmeal Bread

1 lb wheatmeal
½ lb barley meal
1 teaspoon dried yeast dissolved with one teaspoon honey or molasses
2 teaspoons sea salt
1 pint tepid water
METRIC: 450g wheatmeal; 225g barley meal; 575mls tepid water

An alternative barley meal recipe which gives a dark loaf with a nice nutty flavour and a good, close texture. Very good for toast, or as a base for open sandwiches.

Mix the frothed yeast into the flours. Knead very thoroughly (this is a lovely dough which leaves a slight film on the hands due to the wetness of barley).
Put to rise for a longer time and in a warmer place than usual. Knock back, knead again, place in tins or bake as a round on a greased baking sheet, or as rolls, leave to rise until doubled in size – again this may take longer than usual. Sprinkle the tops lavishly with cracked wheat, sunflower or sesame seeds, or a mixture of seeds as you wish.

Rye Bread
Bara Rhyg

1½ lbs rye flour
¾ lb plain white strong flour
2 teaspoons dried yeast dissolved with **½ teaspoon honey or molasses in warm water**
2 teaspoons sea salt
1 tablespoon oil
tepid water to mix – approx. 1 pint
METRIC: 675g rye flour; 350g white strong flour; approx. 575mls tepid water

There is no rise in rye, thus all-rye loaves are very dark, dense and flat. This 2 to 1 mixture with white flour is worth trying – cut thin it is good with cheese. In a very much smaller proportion (5 to 1) made to the same method it makes a nice loaf to toast which is again good with cheese. Use as little sugar as possible as rye is sweet-tasting. Rye smells beautiful when it is baking and has a lovely golden crust which contrasts well with the dark interior.

This is a tough dough which benefits from the electric dough hook. But it rises well . . . give it two if you can, before putting in the tins for the final rise.
Smaller loaves bake better than one large one. Make a long centre cut on the tops, sprinkle with rye meal, bake 30 mins in a hot oven, then 30 mins lower down in a moderate oven.

Three Grain Bread

10 ozs plain strong white flour
2 ozs rye flour
1 oz barley flour
1 teaspoon dried yeast dissolved with scant teaspoon honey or molasses in ¼ pint warm water
6 fl ozs tepid water (approx) to mix sesame seeds
METRIC: 275g white flour; 50g rye flour; 25g barley flour; approx. 325mls warm water

This is a recipe for those who like barley, but perhaps not
in such a high proportion as in the Barley Bread recipe.
Even such a small amount as in this one scents and flavours
the bread unmistakably. Very good with cheese.

Mix and warm the flours and dissolve the salt in hot water.
Mix to a dough with the frothed yeast and warm water,
adding the salt last. This is a darling dough to handle, being
very soft and pliable. Give it two rises and
breakdowns if you can before shaping it into a shallow
2lb greased, warmed tin. Cut across the top and sprinkle
with sesame seeds. Bake in a very hot oven for
15 mins, then reduce heat to hot for 15 mins, finally finish
out of the tin for 10 mins in a low oven.

Sunday White Bread
Bara Can

1 lb plain strong unbleached white flour
1 teaspoon dried yeast dissolved with one teaspoon honey or molasses sugar in ¼ pint warm water
1 oz butter
1 egg
2 teaspoons sea salt
7 fl ozs (approx) warm milk
METRIC: 450g flour; 25g sugar; 25g butter; 200mls warm milk

A rich, satisfying loaf with a thin, crisp crust, baked
for special occasions.

Rub the butter into the flour. Add the beaten egg
to the frothed yeast, together with the warm milk and salt.
Pour into a well in the centre of the warmed floor.
Mix with the fingers until a soft dough is formed. Knead
well until the dough is nice and shiny and attractively
yellow in colour. Shape into one large loaf, insert
in greased and floured warmed tin and set to rise in a warm
place for about 1½ hours until twice the original size.
Bake in a hot oven 30 mins, then reduce to
moderate for a further 15 mins.

"'Twas beautiful dough, like a milking breast it was".
Anon.

Maslin Bread
Bara Cymysg

20 oz wheatmeal flour
4 oz rye flour
1 teaspoon dried yeast dissolved with 1 teaspoon honey or molasses in ¼ pint warm water
1 tablespoon vegetable oil
2 teaspoons salt
about ½ pint warm water
METRIC: 575g wheatmeal; 125g rye; 425mls water

Maslin is the name given to bread made from a mixture of grains – usually rye and wheat flour – deriving from early times when the sowing of mixed grain was an insurance against the failure of wheat on its own. At the medieval table maslin bread was for the lower orders. Don't let this put you off, for this version I have developed, using rye and wheatmeal, procedures an addictively delicious close-textured loaf with a slightly malty flavour.

Mix the warmed flours together, make a well in the centre and pour in the frothed yeast, topped up with the rest of the water and the dissolved salt. Knead and set to raise until double in size. Knock back, knead lightly what is now a very pleasant, pliable dough, shape into a greased and floured 3 lb loaf tin, or one 2lb and one 1lb tin. Cover and leave to rise again, about 40 minutes. Bake 15 minutes in a hot oven, then reduce to moderate for a further 21-30 minutes depending on the size of loaf.

Soda & Buttermilk Breads

Bakestone Bread
Bara Planc

1 lb plain white strong flour
½ teaspoon sea salt
1 teaspoon bicarbonate of soda
½ pint buttermilk
METRIC: 450g plain flour; 275mls buttermilk

The bakestone was often pressed into service to make a quick loaf, sometimes with a yeast dough taken from the main batch on baking day, but equally often with a dough employing another raising agent, as in this recipe, which I find easier to manage on the bakestone than a yeast dough. The ability to make a quick loaf on the bakestone is a useful acquisition, but it is not easy, and mastering the knack a salutory lesson in appreciating the skills of earlier cooks.

Add the salt to the flour, dissolve the soda in the buttermilk and mix gradually into the flour to form a soft dough. Knead lightly and turn on to a floured board. Shape into a round, flattening the top with a rolling pin. The bakestone must be well greased and not too hot or the loaf will burn on the outside before it is done inside. Cook both sides to a golden brown.

Pikelets
Bara Pyglyd

1 lb plain strong white flour
1 teaspoon dried yeast
½ pint milk with ½ pint water mixed
1 dessertspoon sea salt
1 teaspoon sugar
2 tablespoons oil
METRIC: 450g flour; 275mls milk + 275mls water

The English name is thought to be a corruption of the Welsh. 'Pitchy bread' was another name for these yeast pancakes which resemble the thicker English crumpet (cooked in rings) in their mixture. But most of the more recent recipes in Wales have become muddled with the pancake and lightcake recipes and are egg and soda mixes. The Welsh love holey griddle breads and cakes, for the holes are capable of holding so much lovely golden butter.

Warm flour in low oven 5 mins. Warm oil, milk/water, sugar to blood heat − use a little to cream the yeast. Add salt to warmed flour, make a batter with the yeasty liquid. Beat it very well until quite smooth. Cover bowl and leave to rise at room temperature 1½-2 hours until well up the bowl and covered with bubbles. Beat down with a spoon, cover again and leave to recover 30 mins in a warm place. Cook pikelets one at time (about 6in across) on a lightly-greased moderately hot griddle. The holes appear very quickly. Cook both sides to a pale brown colour.

Sweet Breads

Wholewheat Scones

1 lb plain white flour
8 ozs wholewheat flour
5 ozs margarine or butter
3 ozs sugar
pinch salt
2 teaspoons bicarbonate of soda
4½ teaspoons cream of tartar
¾ pint milk to make a soft dough
METRIC: 450g plain flour; 225g wholewheat flour; 425mls milk 150g margarine or butter; 75g sugar

Sift the flours together and lightly rub in the fat,
sift in the raising agents and salt and mix well. Add all the
milk at once to make a soft dough. Knead lightly to make
smooth, roll out ½-¾in thick, cut out, brush with
egg or milk and bake in a hot oven about 20 mins.

Barley Scones

8 ozs S.R. flour
4 ozs barley meal
½ teaspoon bicarbonate of soda
¼ teaspoon cream of tartar
pinch salt
1 egg
4 ozs lard
2 ozs sugar
milk or buttermilk to mix to a stiff dough
METRIC: 225g S.R. flour; 125g barley meal; 125g lard; 50g sugar

Cream the sugar and lard, then beat the egg well and beat into the creamed mixture. Add the mixed flours by degrees until a stiff dough is obtained, using a little milk or buttermilk if necessary. Cut in rounds and bake in a very hot oven for about 15 minutes.

Wholewheat Currant Bread
Bara Cyrens

1 lb wholewheat flour
2 ozs currants
1 teaspoon dried yeast
1 teaspoon honey or molasses dissolved together in a little warm water
1 teaspoon salt
8 fl. ozs milk and water (warm)
METRIC: 450g wholewheat flour; 63g currants; 250ml milk and water

A special-occasion bread made in Wales at Christmas and New Year, or for harvest suppers.

Mix the currants with the flour and make into dough in the usual way with the frothed yeast. Knead well, put to rise, knock back and knead again, lightly, then shape into tins and leave to rise until the dough reaches the top of the tins. Bake in a hot oven about 40 minutes.

Bara Brith

1 lb wheatmeal flour
1 teaspoon yeast
2 ozs brown molasses sugar
3 ozs butter, cut and melted into
¼ pint milk
3 ozs seedless raisins
3 ozs currants
1 oz candied peel
1 teaspoon salt
1 teaspoon mixed spice
METRIC: 450g flour; 50g sugar; 75g each butter, raisins & currants; 25g candied peel

The famous speckled (with fruit) bread of Wales. Good *bara brith* is a yeast bread made with wholewheat or wheatmeal flour (more recent recipes have turned into a cake). The fruit should be worked into the dough during its second kneading. Serve cut and buttered in thin slices.

Keep everything warm. Cream the yeast with a little of the warm milk, then add to the warmed flour and salt. Work into a dough with the warm milk.
Set to rise until doubled in bulk – about an hour.
Knock back, work in the sugar, spices and fruit, aiming for even distribution. Insert into warmed and buttered loaf tin (3 pint), leave to rise to top of tin (about 40 mins) Bake 20-30 mins in the centre of a hot oven, covering the top with paper or foil for the final 10 mins. Leave to cool a little before turning out. Brush top with sugar syrup to glaze. For a richer loaf, increase the butter and sugar as required.

Pembrokeshire Yeast Buns
Migiod sir Benfro

1½ lbs wheatmeal flour
1 pkt 'easy-blend' dried yeast
3 ozs brown molasses sugar
2 ozs butter
2 ozs currants and sultanas
1 oz candied peel
½ pint milk to mix
pinch salt
1 egg
METRIC: 675g flour; 75g sugar; 50g butter; 50g currants and sultanas; 25g candied peel; 275mls milk

These buns were a traditional part of the Pembrokeshire New Year celebrations They are best eaten warm, and though the tradition is to use white flour, I think they are much nicer made from wheatmeal flour, and for this recipe I used the new 'easy-blend' dried yeast which is not mixed first with water but mixed dry into the flour before adding the liquid.

Warm the flour. Rub in the butter. Beat the egg and add to warm milk, stir salt, sugar, yeast and dried fruits into the flour. Make a well in the centre, pour in the liquid, mix well and knead. Set in a warm place to prove for an hour. Cut into 18 rounds, place well apart on greased baking sheets, set to rise until double in size (30 mins), then bake in a hot oven for 15-20 mins. Brush with honey to glaze.

Caraway Seed Bread
Bara Carawe or Bara Hadau

10 ozs wheatmeal flour
2 ozs rolled oats
2 ozs bacon fat or 1 tablespoon vegetable oil in ½ pint warm water
1 sachet 'easy-blend' yeast
2 ozs molasses sugar or honey
1 teaspoon salt
1 teaspoon caraway seed
METRIC: 275g flour; 50g rolled oats; 50g fat; 275 mls warm water; 50g sugar or honey

This recipe for a caraway seed loaf, rather than
a cake, which is still very popular in rural Wales, is adapted
from the one given in 'Y Tŷ, a'r Teulu' ('The House,
and Domestic Economy')1891, which Mrs Bessie Jones of
Lampeter kindly translated for me. Again I have used the
new 'easy-blend' yeast.

Warm the flour and rolled oats, mixed together.
Add the salt and the sugar and caraway seed, lastly the
yeast. Make a well in the centre, pour in the warm water
and fat or oil, mix all together into a dough. Knead for a
few minutes on a floured board, then set to rise for
about an hour in a warm place. Knock back, then insert
into a shallow 2-pint greased, warm loaf tin, make a cut
down the centre, sprinkle top with rolled oats or mixed
seeds and bake in a moderate oven about 40 mins,
when the top should be a lovely deep golden brown.
This makes a nice sweet bread for tea and an unusual
accompaniment for a mature cheese.

Gingerbread
Bara Sinsir

½ lb plain flour
6 ozs brown molasses sugar
4 ozs butter
6 ozs black treacle
2 ozs chopped mixed peel
½ teaspoon cream of tartar
5 fl ozs milk
½ teaspoon bicarbonate soda
METRIC: 225g flour; 175g sugar; 125g butter; 175g treacle; 50g mixed peel; 150mls milk

Though we know it today more as a cake, gingerbread began as biscuits made from a paste of grated stale bread, ginger, sugar and spices. But why or how was ginger left out of this traditional Welsh recipe, which I found first under the title: 'Old Welsh Gingerbread' with the explanation that it used to be sold at the old Welsh fairs. Was ginger forgotten because so obvious an ingredient, or is it really meant to represent gingerbread without actually containing the spice? Because it does in fact have a gingery taste!

Warm the treacle slightly so it will mix with the milk. Sift the flour and raising agents together and rub in the butter. Add sugar and peel, stir in the treacle and milk. Bake in a shallow, greased tin for 1½ hours in a medium oven.

Oatcakes
Bara Ceirch

In Wales, oatcakes were most often made on the bakestone, but sometimes on the iron shelves of an oven, when a special wooden paddle (*crafell*) was used for putting them in and taking them out.

Welsh oatcakes traditionally were huge — 'big as dinner-plates' is a recurring comparison, then and now — and thin to the point of transparency. Making them was a skilled operation, as I found to my chagrin. Having failed to 'palm' mine to more than 8 inches across, I went, humbly, to Lampeter, to watch 95-year-old Mrs Davies make them 10 inches across at least. Without the aid of a rolling pin or anything other than her deft hands. She worked a pile of spreading oatcakes under each hand simultaneously, growing larger by the minute, the edges kept firm by an alternating up-ending rolling on the table, dexteriously held in pairs between her palms. Hard to describe — I was grateful for the lesson, but no better at achieving that splendid size.

Take Mrs Davies' daughter's advice (who cannot achieve the size either) and cravenly fall back on the use of that modern gadget — the rolling pin.

Whichever way they are to be flattened, the oatmeal is kneaded first with skim milk or water, or as in the second recipe, with a little bacon fat, or vegetable oil, until it holds together as a dough. This is quite hard work and takes up to 10 minutes.

It is essential to use the correct medium grade of oatmeal — too coarse a meal and the dough will not hold properly, too fine and it will be sticky.

Break the dough off in balls and flatten them on an oatmeal-strewn board. Sprinkle oatmeal on top and add another flattened ball. Continue to make in as big a pile as you can manage until the oatcakes are as large and thin as possible, holding the edges firm by working against a cupped hand.

Bake on a medium bakestone, or on a baking sheet in a medium oven. Usually on the bakestone the oatcakes were cooked on one side only, then placed standing-up with the unbaked side towards the fire. They kept for months in an air-tight container: often a whole day would be set aside for baking them in Mrs Davies' day.

The use of the word *bara* (bread) and not *cacen* or *teisen* (cake) in the Welsh is indicative of their importance as a staple bread in Wales.

Recipe 1.

Medium-grade oatmeal, quantity depending upon how many oatcakes you wish to make, say, 1 lb.

Skim milk or water to mix.

Put the oatmeal in a bowl, moisten with milk or water and mix with a wooden spoon initially. When a dough is formed, knead with the hands, adding more liquid until the dough feels pliable. Then proceed to make the oatcakes as described.

Oatcakes

These small quantities are explained
by the advisability of mixing and rolling out only a few
oatcakes at a time, before the mixture hardens.
This is the recipe I prefer.

Heat the fat in the water. Sprinkle the oatmeal on to it,
kneading well. Flour a board with oatmeal, roll the
dough out very thinly to about 10 inches in diameter if you
can manage it. Bake for about 5-10 minutes on a
moderately hot bakestone, one side only. Stand up against
the fire to harden the other side.

WELSH WHEAT STOOK, FROM THE
DRAWING BY LADY LLANOVER IN
'GOOD COOKERY', 1867

Glazes

A variety of glazes can be employed to enhance the appearance of these breads, though some will argue for leaving the crust as it naturally develops. It's a matter of choice.

A salt-water wash will strengthen the crust; beaten egg will give a good, deep gloss; egg white alone a shine; milk will deepen the colour.

Honey or sugar and water wash will give a sticky, shiny finish to sweet buns and breads.

Salt and sugar washes are best brushed on when bread is still hot from the oven; egg and milk glazes should go on just before the bread goes in the oven.

The flours which have been used in preparing these recipes are:

Felin Geri: 100% stoneground wholewheat flour
Plain white unbleached stoneground flour

The Mill at Whitemill: 100% stoneground wholewheat

Mrs Horsefield's: organically-grown whole-germ Welsh barley flour

---

Mayall's Pimhill: 100% stoneground organically-grown wholewheat flour.
100% stoneground organically-grown rye flour.
85% stoneground organically-grown wheatmeal flour.

Y Felin, St Dogmeals: 100% stoneground wholewheat Welsh flour.
85% stoneground wheatmeal Welsh flour.
Unbleached stoneground white Welsh flour.

'Spiller's': 'Harvest Gold' Wheatmeal Strong Plain
   Flour (85%)

'Tesco's': own brand 100% stoneground wholewheat flour.
   Own brand strong plain flour Brown Wheatmeal.
   Own brand strong plain white unbleached flour.

Loose, stoneground flours and meals (source not always
identified) and seeds from 'Herbs and Beans', Kings Road,
Cardiff.

OVEN TEMPERATURES

Slow	240° – 310°F	115° – 155°C	¼ – 2
Moderate	320° – 370°F	160° – 190°C	3 – 4
Fairly Hot	380° – 400°F	195° – 205°C	5
Hot	410° – 440°F	210° – 230°C	6 – 7
Very Hot	450° – 480°F	235° – 250°C	8 – 9

Breadmaking note:
In Wales, as elsewhere, a handful of oatmeal was
often added to a white flour bread dough to enhance its
texture, flavour and food value – not too much or
the bread will be heavy. In fact, a little oatmeal is an
improvement to almost any bread recipe and
well worth experimentation.

In this series

1. A Book of Welsh Bread
2. A Book of Welsh Country Cakes and Buns
3. A Book of Welsh Bakestone Cookery
4. A Book of Welsh Country Puddings and Pies
5. A Book of Welsh Fish
6. A Book of Welsh Soups and Savouries

Also by Bobby Freeman

Lloyd George's Favourite Dishes (1974, 1976, 1978—Ed.)
Gwent—A Guide to South East Wales (1980)
First Catch Your Peacock—A Book of Welsh Food (1980)
Welsh Country House Cookery (1983)
Welsh Country Cookery—Traditional Recipes from the Country Kitchens of Wales (Y Lolfa, 1987)

First impression: 1981
Revised and reprinted: 1983
Reprinted (Y Lolfa): 1987
Reprinted (Y Lolfa): 1993
Reprinted (Y Lolfa): 2001

ISBN 0 83243 137 9

Printed and published in Wales by
Y Lolfa Cyf., Talybont, Ceredigion SY24 5AP
tel (01970) 832 304 *fax* 832 782 *isdn* 832 813
e-mail ylolfa@ylolfa.com *internet* www.ylolfa.com

Please send for our free full-colour catalogue!